Thank you, God, for the people who love me.

Thank you for Mum and Dad
who look after me.

Thank you for people
who play with me.

Thank you for babies
They are sweet!

Thank you for people who help me.

Thank you for friends.

Thank you for all the people
who love me.